*Presented To:*

..............................................

*From:*

..............................................

# DECRYPTO
## Unlock Your Life Journey

Your Key To The Mystery Of Boundless Happiness:
A Step By Step Inspirational Guide

BY LINDA K. FORD

# Decrypto
*Unlock Your Life Journey*

by Linda K. Ford

ISBN: 978-0-6482990-0-4 (Paperback)
ISBN: 978-0-6482990-1-1 (eBook)

Published 2018 by Linda K. Ford: www.lindakfordauthor.com
© Copyright 2018. All rights reserved.

Except for the purpose of fair reviewing, no part of this publication may be reproduced or transmitted in any form or by any means, electronic or mechanical, including photocopying, recording or any information storage and retrieval system, without prior written permission from the publisher.

*Cover artwork "Blind Love" by Jena DellaGrottaglia, used under license: www.autumnsgoddess.com*

*Illustrations and design by Intrepid Sparks: www.intrepidsparks.com*

# *Note to the Reader*

This book was written to assist you on the pathway to create the life of your choice.

My wish is that, throughout this book you gain insight and courage to explore hidden aspects of yourself and a deeper understanding of your emotions, yourself, and your everyday life. With increased clarity, you will be able to see a new vision for the future and be equipped to move forward to create the change that you desire but have not yet reached. I have included positive reflections and affirmations at the beginning of each chapter, to support you on this journey.

Magic is possible when you can clearly see the opportunities that were always there beside you. I wish you peace and serenity in your everyday life and bucket-loads of joy and passion to fuel your dreams into manifestation.

*LK Ford*

# *Contents*

Introduction: How it All Started.....................3

1. The Search................................9
2. Footprints in the Sand......................13
3. A Reflection on Emotions....................19
4. The Eye of Reality .........................29
   - *Discover the Hidden You* ........................31
   - *Starting A Journal* ............................32
5. The Blank Canvas...........................37
   - *Letting Go of Emotional Blocks*..................42
   - *Sarah's Childhood*............................43
6. Defeat....................................47
   - *Sam's Experience of Defeat* .....................49
7. Inaccuracies of Thought .....................57
   - *Mental versus Physical Tiredness*.................61
   - *Strategies to Deal with Emotions* ................63
   - *Find Out What Works for You* ..................64
8. To Observe or Participate ....................69
   - *Stephen's Experience* ..........................69
   - *Mindfulness—Walking Meditation*...............72
   - *To Be in a Place of Stillness or Quietness*.........73
9. The Will ..................................77
   - *Jane's Battle* ..................................78

10. The Void ............................................... 83
   - *Carol Breaks Free* ............................... 85
   - *Redefine Yourself and Reassess Your Life* ........ 87
11. Diving Deep ........................................... 91
   - *The Little You* .................................. 95
   - *Praise Yourself and Give Focus to the Positive* ... 98
   - *Innocence* ....................................... 99
12. Inherited Legacies .................................... 103
   - *Working with Children* ........................... 105
13. Emotions and Health .................................. 115
14. Leave the Past Behind ................................ 121
15. Relinquish and Rechoose .............................. 127
   - *How You Can Use This Method* .................... 128
   - *How to Start* ................................... 129
   - *Sarah's Outcome* ................................ 136
16. The Power of Manifesting ............................. 141
17. Dream Big ............................................ 149
   - *Create a Dream Catcher* ......................... 151
   - *Empower Positive Thought* ....................... 152
About The Author ......................................... 156

# Introduction
# *How it All Started*

As a small child in a town in England, I peered out at the white snowflakes that swirled to the earth. The ground swiftly became covered with thick snow, which mesmerized me and ignited my curiosity. I sought to understand this marvel of life, which provided some solace from the noise and general commotion of family living.

As a young child, I felt swallowed up by the intensity of my world. I was born into a crowd; I am the ninth child out of a family of ten children.

Early in life, I learned to extend my senses and awareness to perceive what was happening in my busy family. I found that I could connect to my family's energy and thoughts in order to discover what they were feeling, which enabled me to determine what I should do next. I learned to read them, to see behind what they portrayed.

We emigrated to Australia and then to New Zealand when I was between four and six years old. I had two children, Mathew and Nicole, in my early twenties. In their preteen years, I sold my home, bought a yacht, and embarked on a sailing adventure from New Zealand to England.

I enjoyed sailing to far and distant shores, which in turn widened my vision of life. This experience roused my curiosity from its slumber, where it had dug itself underground and lay dormant and inactive. The philosopher and the theoretician within me sprang into life. I relished the differences between countries and cultures.

The experience drew me to question the meaning of my life. I returned to New Zealand after this spectacular adventure for family reasons.

My yacht, Ebony, was sold in England, and it quickly became apparent that my choice to go on this sailing voyage had created major repercussions not just for myself but also for some of my family.

At the time, my life seemed to crumble beneath me. I was sent into emotional turmoil, experiencing major guilt, grief, and betrayal. This new reality left me floundering in the sea of life. I had made a choice that had a consequence, and the effect of this choice prompted me to form a wall of defense around me. It wasn't until a later stage in my life that I was able to dismantle this wall, brick by brick.

This marked the beginning of a search to heal my life, and it was also the beginning of my research into the intricacies of the mind. This search for answers was not only for myself but for others too.

I was introduced to a visionary woman, an intuitive speaker who supported me on this journey. My task was to unwind the intricate weave that entwined me and my life—a product of the influence of my past. This brought about the birth and discovery of the healer within me.

I decided to enroll at Canterbury University in New Zealand to study social work. I later worked in the mental health field, supporting individuals who experienced mental illness.

I quickly recognized that for many of those I met,

the past had created scars. Their wounds were deep, and this increased my determination to find a quick, gentle way to support people in healing their lives.

## *The Healer*

Over the years, I developed and refined techniques that enable me to link mentally to a person, my mind to their mind. I can then feel within me what the other person feels, and I can decrypt the thoughts connected to their emotions.

First, I link to the person's present-day thoughts and feelings. Then I work my way through the energetic layers to decipher and unravel the root cause behind the individual's situation.

If you look into the night sky, the stars twinkle and shine. They are so far away, and yet they seem almost touchable. The energetic layers within you mirror this sense of expansion; they are vast and far-reaching. It is almost like sending a rocket to reach one of the twinkling stars.

I mentally push through the energetic layers to locate the core of the problem within the person, which is often at a very deep level. The patterns and themes behind their emotions become clear, as does how all this manifests in the present.

I then facilitate healing by shifting the energy and emotion from the person at all levels. This energy moves through my body; the energy generally moves upwards. The healer within me heals the area worked on in order to harmonize the person's heart, mind, and body.

The process creates a greater sense of ease and peace within the person and the energy in the physical body. In turn, it endows greater awareness and clarity to the person's mind, increasing motivation and energy in order to move and create positive change.

I can feel the person's emotions and thoughts change into a new vision of life. We then talk about what has to be done to create the desired change and discuss how to empower and strengthen new, positive choices into being.

*A long time ago, a spark of an idea grew like a tiny seedling, weak and spindly. I turned it to the sun and the sea for inspiration. As the years passed, it blossomed and then wilted. At times, it lay waiting for me to have the courage to put words onto paper.*

# Chapter One
## *The Search*

The knowledge within this book is born from an expansive curiosity and a strong, unrelenting drive that has propelled me on a search to unravel the ties that bind people. At every corner stood obstacles, which increased my determination to discover more.

I studied myself and those around me, and I gained vast knowledge and insight by working for many years in community mental health and through my intuitive healing practice. The knowledge I acquired and pass on to you will take you on an adventure into the layers and depths of your subconscious mind, your inner world.

We live in the physical world, yet we are influenced by a parallel world of energy within each of us. This is multilayered, complex, and unique to each individual. Your life is influenced by the mental, emotional, spiritual, and hereditary ties that bind. We emanate energy and create certain potential for the future. This potential is like a seed planted in the psyche. If nurtured and given the right conditions, it will grow.

The healer is the decrypto, your guide. Decrypt is a generic term that means to decipher. Put simply, it means to unscramble a message. The root prefix, crypto, is from the Greek kryptos, meaning hidden or secret. That is what this book sets out to do: to teach you how to unscramble the hidden messages that we all hold within us.

To learn how to decrypt yourself, is to ultimately find yourself. It is like putting together a puzzle. It takes time for the pieces to be interlinked and the picture to become clear.

If you look closely, hidden keys can be found everywhere as other people display the issues you seek to resolve within yourself. They will mirror your subconscious programming, bring you understanding, and allow you to see a reflection of what is inside of you.

With this knowledge comes power, which allows the veils of secrecy that can cloud your vision to fall. You will see that you do have options and opportunities to make different choices in life. This in itself strengthens your courage to walk free from the past and move forward to create your goals and dreams.

Does this seem like an impossible task? I am here to tell you it is within your reach. Knowledge is the key because understanding brings clarity. With clarity, real change can occur.

*Daytime activity is a reflection of your actual mind. That is why it can be easy to know your subconscious mind, because you are acting it out - living the thoughts from it.*

# Chapter Two
# *Footprints in the Sand*

*This short story, Footprints in the Sand, is an introduction to how individual perception is changeable depending on one's mind-set at any given time...*

It has been raining for most of the night. The early morning looks dull and lifeless, with dark clouds and low fog. I woke with a sense of boredom that gnawed at my insides. I thought about what to do with my day. After working a full week, one would think I would be happy to relax and enjoy my time at home. I decided to take a walk along the beach to shake away this lethargy and clear my mind. What exactly was this inner boredom? Was it merely an illusion of the mind?

While walking across the road over the sand dunes onto the beach and looking out to sea, I smiled. Maybe the answer to my question lay somewhere out there. I looked closely at the intricate patterns forming on the windswept sand to see that art was all around me.

A light drizzle began to fall, and so I decided to head home. I unintentionally retraced my footprints in the sand. Suddenly, I realized I was walking over my past; the past and the present were crossing. My footprints marked the firm sand—but for how long? They were soon swept away by the tide, leaving no trace of what was there except for my own memory of this time. A strange feeling arose with the realization that the present so quickly becomes the past.

Raindrops made crazy patterns on my glasses, obscuring the way ahead and emphasizing that with impaired visibility, one doesn't see things clearly. At that point, I could only see so much of my surroundings. Many elements around me were still there but no longer visible.

I realized that if you can't see what is truly happening in your life, you will make decisions without being aware of all relevant facts. Opportunities may go unseen as your mind creates a form of blindness to what is truly happening. Your past obscures your vision, creating inaccuracies of thought, and the same pattern can be repeated.

A belief that opportunities are limited creates limited opportunities. How many people have walked this beach today and formed totally different conclusions? Each of us takes an individual journey, and even when we walk the same route, our experiences will be totally different.

I unlocked the back door to my home, and as I hastily took off my coat to put thoughts onto paper, I realized the feeling of boredom had dissipated. This was purely a mindset in that moment. Old patterns are often retraced routinely, and you will continue to bring the past into the present.

Not only does the present cross the past, but it merges with the past to become the present. We follow patterns of reasoning and behavior through a process of induction and embrace the false security to be found in the certainty of result.

As I start to write, I look outside towards the estuary, which is still covered with thick fog. My mind, now alert and in a creative mood, sees this as mysterious, not dull and dreary as before.

There is potential for description, which fills me with an inner excitement. I have created two different realities within the same landscape!

The lesson learnt on this short journey is a tool to support you in everyday life. If you have negative feelings, or if something upsets you, acknowledge what has come up for you.

Think about how you can change your focus to see your present situation in an alternative way. The key is deciding to become more creative in your thinking and in everyday life. The power is in your hands, if you decide to take it.

## *Notes*

*I search the sea for inspiration and realize that creativity has to be let loose to spread its wings, to soar to the skies!*

# Chapter Three
## *A Reflection on Emotions*

The fin and the back of a whale can be seen gliding just beneath the surface of the ocean. Momentarily, the whale gushes spray from its blowhole. In one glimpse, a tiny flicker of the whale instantly draws attention. Everyone there stands silent, fixed, waiting to be shown more.

While looking out to sea from high up on the balcony, I linger, searching for the whale, and I ask,

"Has the whale dived deep below, into the depths of the ocean?" The image in my mind has faded just as my emotional response has dissolved. I recognize that for my emotional reaction to resurface, it has to wait for a trigger to move it into action, like the whale. On the surface, there is the known, calm blue water, and yet deep within the layers of the ocean, another, unknown world exists, living, breathing, and pulsating with life!

This is very similar to the states of the conscious and subconscious mind. You can only tell what is shown to you, the parts that surface up through the mind, allowing the emotions to be seen.

The known is the conscious world, and the unknown is the subconscious world. You have a life that goes on beneath the surface of what you portray yourself to be. Like the unknown depths of the ocean, it's pulsating with energy, but it's unseen and unknown until energy and thought are driven to the surface, to be perceived by the conscious mind.

How much attention do you give these inner signals when they surface during your everyday life? Do they dive back into the depths of you to become once again submerged, or do you dig deeper, look more closely, and pull on the thread that connects to what lies below, in order to decrypt some hidden truth?

Recollections of the past come into the present on a regular basis, almost seeking validation. It takes only one thought to rise to the conscious mind during a conversation or randomly surface during the day to trigger a past memory of a similar event. Some thoughts are stamped indelibly within the mind. The energy and emotion connected to them is noticed first. It can roar fiercely like an angry lion, forcing the mind and body into emotional submission. The thoughts and the energy content from the past feed your reaction to what is happening now.

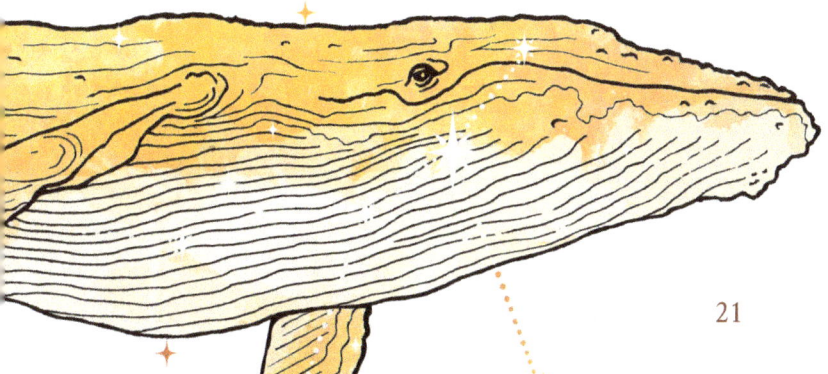

Normally the memory may glow like a small ember, unless you fuel the fire by inadvertently raising it. The memory will fan the fire until it rages high and flickers wildly, causing strong emotional surges to be felt and relived. When the fuel of the emotion is spent, the sensations dwindle, often leaving regret, sadness, and sorrow. You may then ask yourself, "What is wrong with me, and why did I act in that way?"

If you reflect on this, if you dive below the surface to unravel what is really happening for you, then the hidden, subconscious thoughts will be brought back again to the conscious mind and may be resolved. You can only make peace with what you know.

It is through your interactions with others that you can see reflections of what is within you. They can act as a catalyst to bring to your conscious awareness the fact that they have thoughts, patterns, and expectations that are similar to your own.

A glimmer of the whale can again be seen sliding along, just beneath the surface of the deep ocean. The whale had fooled me into believing it had swum away, and yet all along it was still there. This reflects a similarity to emotions, which lie hidden just beneath the surface. We may not be constantly aware of them, but they are there. You always have a choice between allowing the past to dominate the present, or to put out the flame of submission and overcome negative aspects of your past.

Emotions are very much like the ocean, which can be calm, still, and seemingly motionless. Then the next minute, they are fanned into life and become turbulent and unyielding. You may feel incapable of escape until the thoughts and the emotions lose their force, and their hold loosens. Eventually, the mind and body will relax and ease until the next time, and you allow a pattern of a past experience to dominate current expectations.

If you frequently connect to the same emotional experience, the emotional impact intensifies over time and can become difficult for you to handle. The engraving of the memory inside the mind becomes deeper. Today's triggers can then appear too difficult for you to master if you believe that you have no control over your emotional experience.

In this case, you will be held captive by your own emotions and will be stuck in the center of a recurrent emotional typhoon. You will not be the captain of your own ship. All strong negative emotions have a root cause, and they can only have an end when you seek to understand what is behind the emotion and is continuing to fuel it.

So I ask you, what lies within you, seeking acknowledgment and recognition?

## *Characteristics of Emotions*

Emotion is energy, and each emotion has unique characteristics. Anger, as you feel it, is often suppressed under layers of defense. It creates negativity on the physical, mental, and emotional levels. Anger can lie on the surface, and beneath this is sadness in some people. Others have sadness on the surface and anger underneath. Some people project their anger outward at others, whereas others hold onto their anger and stew over the past.

Fear also has a debilitating effect on the mind and body, affecting all levels. It can cause a person to withdraw and feel tense and uncomfortable, and this can cause confusion of thought.

Sadness can be a dominant energy in some people. Like tiredness, it can wrap the brain and the mind in a fog, which is the end result of the emotion. If you think back to an experience of a very foggy day, you will not have been able to see very far in front of you. As you know, fog has the ability to cover things in its path, and items appear to be invisible until the fog shifts and moves away.

With sadness, it is like you are inside a fog. It shrouds all your senses and impacts your ability to connect to joy, suppressing positive emotions by dampening them down. It can create an illusion of physical tiredness, affecting memory and your ability to motivate yourself. You become lost in the fog of this emotional feeling.

Calling up and making peace with your past will strengthen your stability, build a sense of peace, and bring you sound quality of life.

# Notes

# A Reflection on Emotions

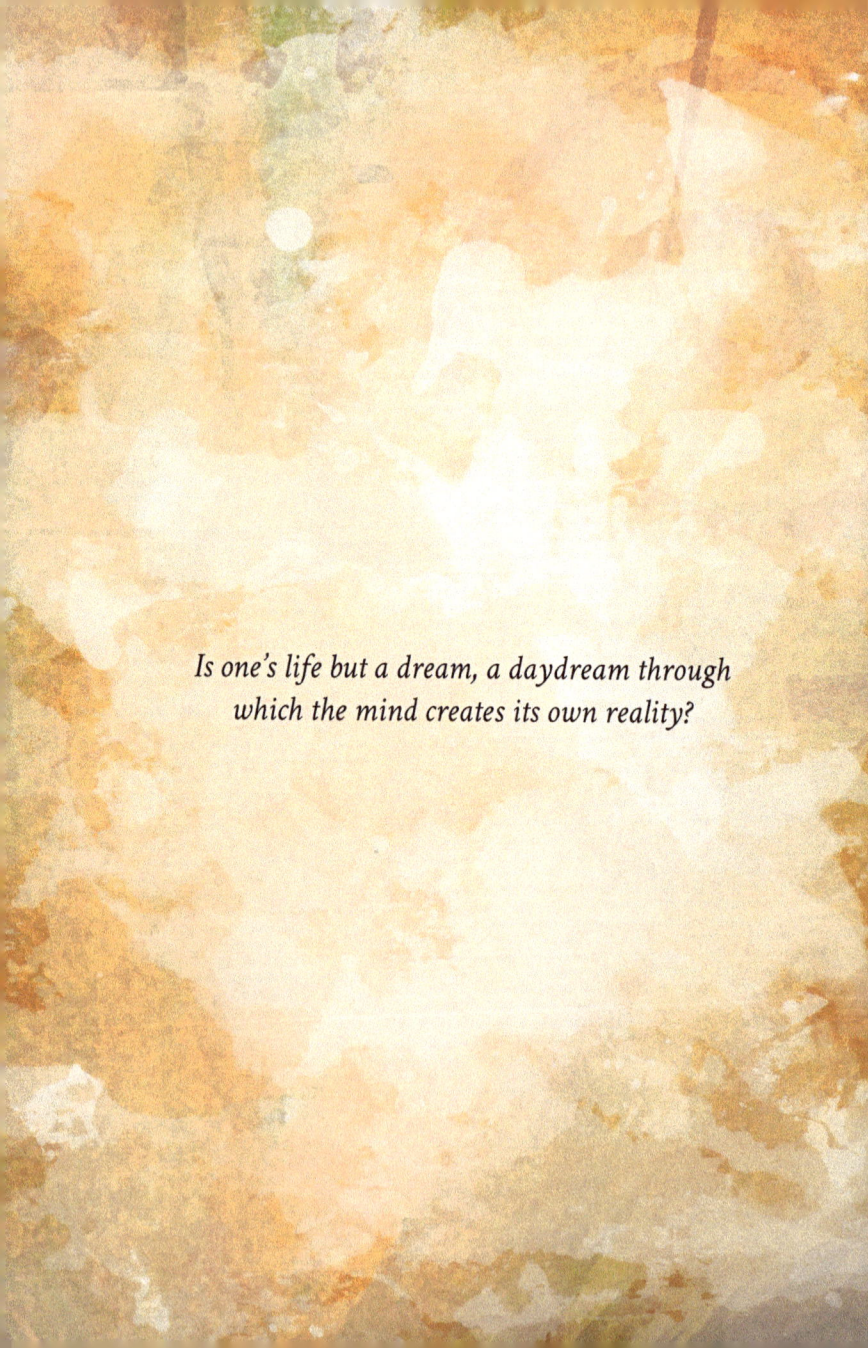

*Is one's life but a dream, a daydream through which the mind creates its own reality?*

# Chapter Four
# *The Eye of Reality*

I enjoy being stirred by different perspectives on 'reality', this quote from the late, Erich Fromm, U.S. psychoanalyst and social philosopher, fits nicely with this chapter. *'Our conscious motivations, ideas, and beliefs are a blend of false information, biases, irrational passions, rationalizations, prejudices, in which morsels of truth swim around and give the reassurance albeit false, that the who mixture is real and true. The thinking processes attempt to organize the*

*whole cesspool of illusions according to the laws of plausibility. This level of consciousness is supposed to reflect reality; it is the map we use for organizing our life.'*

**Fromm, Erich. To Have or to Be? The Nature of the Psyche. (Continuum International Publishing Group, 2005).**

Reality is all about your perception of what feels real and tangible. Your everyday life is a reflection of your mind. It can be easy to know your subconscious mind because you live out your thoughts. You are not separate from the past because everything you have lived through is interwoven into your unique personality.

The outcome of every event has an effect on you, developing a certain emphasis in your mental outlook and emotional well-being. Events can strengthen the attraction of a particular choice or weaken it. The past influences how you will react and experience the present and the future.

If you look at a hand-woven rug, you will see that it has fibers of different colors that bring emphasis to certain areas in the rug. You are the weaver of your own artwork, yet it is not set in concrete; once completed, it can be changed and modified. It is a weave in perpetual motion—never stagnant, always changing. There will be times when the threads in the weave, which represent your life, become entangled. Then the pattern loses creativity, and stagnation occurs.

During these times, you may feel that you are unable to change your situation, yet you can still create positive change in your life. However, this can occur only by exerting positive reflection and matching it with an awareness of what is truly happening, as well as a strong desire to change.

Are you brave enough to make a choice to look at the influence that you can have over your life's direction?

## *Discover the Hidden You*

Many of us reflect quite naturally in our day-to-day lives, pondering on what has happened in our day, our relationships, our work place, friendships, and emotional responses. However, when we consciously make the decision to become more observant in regard to ourselves, we notice these details even more.

## *Starting A Journal.*

When I began 'a search' to understand myself and my life, I found it extremely supportive to keep a journal. I also kept a separate journal for positive affirmations, things that inspired me, new choices and changes that I planned to make in my life.

I would like to encourage you to start your own journal. I understand that life can get busy, however, you will find that creating a small amount of time to note things down during the day will prove to be an invaluable record for you.

For the purpose of your journal, you are looking for clues to enable you to understand yourself on a deeper level. As you read through the chapters in *Decrypto*, you will gain further knowledge and insight to support you on this life-changing adventure.

## *Things to Consider:*

- ☉ Take time to be open and mindful to what is happening, both to you personally and in life in general.

- This also means being observant of other people in your life. They are your teachers. At times, you may see a mirror image, as the good and not so good features they display may be within you.

- Whether negative or positive, when viewing your thoughts, feelings, and emotions, pay particular attention to your triggers and your responses. Be mindful of what you say in conversations with others to find key acceptances. What you say is what you believe.

- Are you saying repeatedly: "Life never works for me. My memory is not good. I never get it right. It's always my fault. I'm not good enough."

- Look for emerging patterns: do you feel powerless, unheard, not valued, or caught in the middle?

- Assess where you are in life. Are you feeling happy, moving forward, feeling stuck, or confused?

- Think about what you are avoiding. Are you using excuses? If so, what are the excuses? For example, "I am too old. I haven't the time. This can't happen for me."

New habits do take time and effort to establish, but the outcome of deciphering yourself will bring many rewards, which will outweigh the effort taken.

## *Notes*

*I'm sitting by the sea in reflection, allowing thoughts to drift and form conclusions. I bring forth new ideas and inspiration, pausing to bask in the serenity of the mind.*

*While I look out on the horizon with the expansive, limitless scene before me, my awareness expands, and I marvel at this beauty. Man and nature walk hand in hand. The simplicity is what brings joy in this moment.*

## Chapter Five
# *The Blank Canvas*

Visualize a canvas painted with a picture that represents your natural abilities and potential. This canvas is stunningly radiant, strong, and vibrant. At an early age, you hide it away because your life experience has caused you to shut down this part of yourself.

This aspect of you seems to disappear from sight, but it's actually always there within you. In order to allow your canvas that represents you to glow with life and inspiration, your uniqueness must be unveiled. To do this means looking deeper at what is preventing you from achieving what you want now.

If you are not creating the life of your choice, you could also consider who or what is standing in your way. Close your eyes and picture yourself being able to achieve one of your life goals right now. Take notice of what is happening with your body. Are you relaxed or tense? What emotions arise when you think about actually achieving what you desire? Visualize yourself there. Think about sensations, tastes, and smells—anything that makes this real for you. This is where your journal will come in handy, to note down your experience.

My passion is sailing, I would imagine myself at the helm of a yacht, scanning the horizon with a steady breeze blowing through my hair and caressing my cheeks. I would feel the warmth of the sun on a cloudless day. I would relish in the tantalizing smell of bread baking in the small gas galley stove. I'd see myself miles away from shore, heading to some strange and foreign land. But how would I initially feel about casting off from the shore at this time in my life, leaving everything behind?

In regard to your visualization, your initial reaction may be happiness. If you focus on this, you may notice that you have an inner resistance, and fear or guilt arises. You may have many excuses for why you cannot reach your goals. Finding reasons why you can't succeed will mean that you won't have to change your ways of thinking and reacting.

Many people never utilize their true potential even though they have the ability and the talent to achieve something really special. They live in the shadows of others and feel disappointed and disillusioned. Accordingly, the door to opportunity that can be freely opened remains closed to them.

I have found that a small change in thinking can create a major life change for some, but for others, this is a much longer process. For some reason, they manage to create the very opposite of what they want to achieve. I liken this to a yacht anchored in a bay that bobs and bounces, moving from side to side, but in fact it stays in the same place. The pivotal point of the anchor keeps the boat moored. Old habits do die hard, and without attention, they will keep you anchored in the same place.

The influences of the ties that bind, as discussed in chapter one, are mental, emotional, spiritual, and hereditary. They can work in your favor or against you. These influences can give you the capability to create success with ease, without necessitating any change on an inner level. This is because the original anchor chain was longer, and it allows more scope to move one's yacht further afield.

It is some people's normal experience to live in positivity, to achieve success, and to manifest all this with little effort. It is their way of living—the opposite of the negativity experienced by the person whose life revolves around sadness, anger, and drama, and who is continually knocked back in life.

You may find that working toward your goals but never taking them through to completion feels safe. If so, is this because you can continue to do so with the security of your old patterns of behavior? The reality, the certainty that you can actually change to create the outcome you desire will mean that you will be faced with the unknown. This can be unsettling, and you may feel vulnerable and uncertain. The parameters within which you have lived your life will begin to shift. There

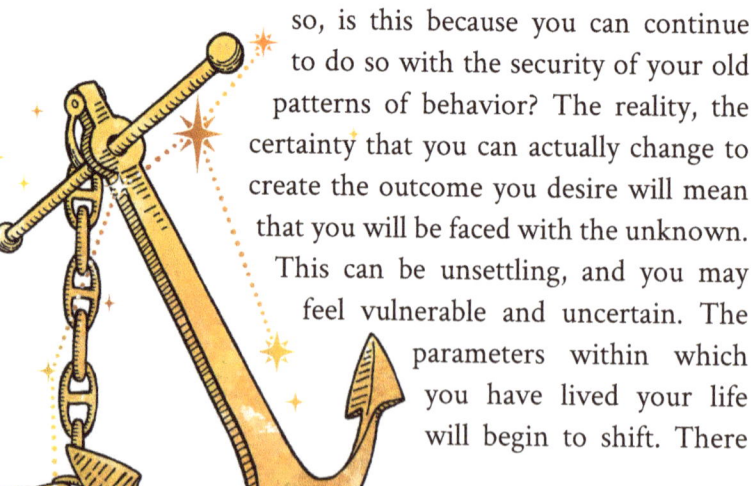

is comfort in what is familiar, and often there's uncertainty with what you don't know.

Once you realize that there is such a wide-open space in which to slip anchor and sail the yacht, you may long to run to a known harbor and hide in the safety of your own entrapment.

While reading this, you might feel that you will be leaving your comfort zone because any change will force you to extend the anchor's chain.

I challenge you to consider that it is not someone or something out there that is creating the things that you do not desire. Instead of life opposing you, you are opposing yourself and standing in your own way.

On an inner level, you unintentionally keep your vibrant canvas hidden because it is not your inner desire to change, and you unconsciously choose to stay as you are and live safely within preset boundaries. If this is the case, you will continue to create obstacles in your own path and block your chances of achieving your aspirations.

At this point, reassess what or who is actually standing in your way and stopping you from moving in the direction of your choice. Consider what you can do to change this.

## *Letting Go of Emotional Blocks*

Emotional blocks are often built in childhood and are perceived by the inner child as a way of protecting oneself. The child builds a defense wall on the subconscious level to surround the pain, numb the experience, and suppress it, with the hope that it will never resurface.

These walls can be so high that at times, you cannot see beyond. What is on the other side remains unseen, untouched, and out of reach, like your canvas. It is like standing in front of a never-ending brick wall. To shift the past is to look at the thoughts and patterns within the bricks, enabling you to take down the walls within your mind.

In everyday life, childhood blocks can have more power over your life than you consciously desire as an adult. As you attempt to push beyond these, the inner child unconsciously resists any attempt to change the original walls of defense.

If the walls are dismantled, it allows freedom of vision, expanding the mind to see the potential for the positive that was hidden on the other side. There is comfort in what is familiar, and there is often uncertainty with what you don't know.

Start slowly and move one brick at a time, by exploring surface thoughts and emotions, until you feel comfortable to let go of more. Be brave and calm yourself.

Reinforce why you desire change. Stand firm with your decision and realize that what you want to achieve is available to you.

## *Sarah's Childhood*

While working with a woman in her late forties, I quickly realized that she had no measure of self-value. Sarah recalled feeling rejected in her early years, and so she developed a belief that she was of low worth and not important. As a child, she did not receive positive feedback, and even when she completed a task well, it was never acknowledged. She could not see any value in herself, and her expectations of herself were for failure.

It was like a glass that reached as far as the sky: no matter what she did, it would never become full. Therefore she could never do enough, and she believed that her best was never good enough. As an adult, she was blinded by this accepted truth. She lived her life to fit her childhood expectations, which was normal for her. The mind was bound by the past, creating conflict.

Sarah had to reeducate the mind and the inner child. She had to choose new acceptances by which to live her life. She had to nurture self-love and learn to place a positive value on herself. This involved acknowledging the good and learning to see the positive in her everyday accomplishments. In making this change, she expected to be treated differently and demanded more out of life. She generally felt much happier in herself.

## *Notes*

*Have you lost your way in the consuming energy of defeat? This will overwhelm you and control you, until one day you realize that there is nothing holding you there other than yourself and the power that you allow your past to exert over you.*

# Chapter Six
## *Defeat*

An acceptance of the inevitability of defeat can totally change your life's direction. Defeat creates disempowerment, a sense of hopelessness often combined with an underlying sadness. There will be a lack of belief in yourself and in your abilities. This weakens the will and gives away your authority and control.

This may be based on an experience during childhood; if so, the adult may not seek to challenge this. You may be unaware of its existence or what is driving it. A child sees the world from a child's perspective, and conclusions made are often inaccurate but endure, buried away.

This causes a contradiction in the mind. Consciously, you will believe you can achieve, yet unconsciously, you have given up before you have even begun. Defeat on an inner level causes you to hold onto, and sink into, the emotional experience; therefore you are held captive by your own emotions. The negative energy dulls the senses and confuses the mind.

The choices and conclusions accepted at that earlier time become what you now live your life by, and they influence your direction, derailing your purpose at every turn. My question to you is this: Are these old choices still valid today? In order to make the change you desire, you have to be in the cockpit of your own yacht. Otherwise, you will be held off course by the whims of your crew, the person you have given your power and control to, while you sit below deck. You won't have full control over the direction you take. Life will seem to control you, and situations will seem beyond your control.

Understanding the causes for feeling defeated and

how it has played out in your life is paramount. Letting go of previously accepted beliefs and reclaiming control and authority of your life will support you in getting back on track. This will enable you to open the door to new opportunities with increased energy and determination.

If you can, think of a question to which you do not know the answer. Your mind will feel blank as you search for the answer and are unable to find it. With defeat, there is no sense of future, no answers, and therefore no direction. You can become stuck in this feeling of defeat, and even though consciously you are ready to move, you will feel constantly held back. The next two chapters will help you to understand your emotional responses and how you can reclaim control over your life. Below outlines how Sam's experience of defeat in his childhood restricts his ability as an adult to create the life of his choice.

## *Sam's Experience of Defeat*

I rented a room at the back of The Best Little Bookshop In Town, close to home in Cronulla, Australia, and started to see people on a casual basis. I was already writing Decrypto at this time, and as the chapters evolved, the people who came to see me mirrored areas I had yet to complete. My main clientele came from word of mouth.

During this time, I also worked with people over the phone, mainly from within Australia and across the ditch in New Zealand. On this particular weekend, there was a festival and the bookshop was open. I decided to put out a sign advertising short healing sessions. A gentleman named Sam was shepherded in by his wife, and he looked a little uncomfortable. I discussed what I did and then connected to him intuitively. At this point, I did not know his history.

When I work with others, I talk to the person about the thoughts, emotions, or images that come to me. Often during these sessions, I have my eyes closed, which allow me to intuit images. I connected to his present-day thoughts, where he felt disillusioned and unhappy. Sam generally felt that he was not heard and his opinions were not valued. At a deeper level, he had a deep sadness, a feeling of powerlessness.

I intuited an image of a small child hiding in the corner of a room. The child was sitting huddled in fear with his head down. There was an image a man present who was pacing around and was angry and abusive. We discussed this in-depth, and Sam disclosed that his father had abused him emotionally and sometimes with harsh physical punishment.

He also talked of the issues he had in his workplace, where he worked hard and believed that he came up with good ideas, however other colleagues always seemed to receive the credit. He felt stuck and was going nowhere, which was a very familiar pattern for him.

I have found during my healing work that a person's present-day situation—for example, the disempowerment felt by Sam—reflects feelings and expectations from childhood. A mirror image energetically pulsates in the subconscious, a pattern of experience with similarities to what is currently happening for him. The experience continues to be reflected on the inner level, even though the trauma may have happened many years before. In Sam's case, the inner child was stuck in the past and remained seated on the floor in a room. He believed he had no control, no way out, which he didn't as a child. It is like someone had left on a movie projector, which replayed the same scene over and over again within the subconscious, as if frozen in time.

I asked Sam how he felt about doing a visualization. By this time, Sam was much more open to this experience, and he said he would give it a go. With his eyes closed, he imagined himself going back in time to when he was a small boy. I encouraged him to visualize himself going to the little him, taking him by the hand, walking through the door, and then closing the door.

This isn't as easy as it may seem; often there is resistance from the inner child, which is felt by the adult. When healing, I can feel within me any resistance in the person, and I intuitively feel any changes in the individual's emotions or energy. I guide people through this process to find out why the inner child doesn't want to move from the corner of the room.

Sam was eventually able to work through this and found it a very emotional but rewarding experience. We then discussed what changes Sam could make in his day-to-day life and how to reinforce positive changes. Sam could see the connection between his past and his part in creating his present situation. For the first time in many years, he felt more settled and stronger, with more clarity and a determination to create a better life for himself and his family.

In understanding the thought and the circumstances that influence the thought, you can more readily change the mind; understanding is the key to healing oneself. Living your new choice completes the healing, and you move forward.

Sam's experience of defeat, gives a clear indication of how his childhood greatly impacted and shaped his life. Take a moment to reflect on your life – have you a story to tell? Has there been an experience of defeat? If the answer is yes, it can be a very sensitive issue on the inner level and it does take a certain amount of bravery to look deeper.

You do have the strength within you, if you decided to unravel your past. Also think about how are you going to reclaim control of your life? Keep notes in your journal and identify the changes you would like to make.

The following **Mantra** is to be repeated seven times a day for seven days.

- ⟲ I breathe in an energy of stillness. *(Take a breath by breathing in through your nose and then out again through your nose or mouth.)*

- ⟲ I breathe in an energy of courage. *(Take a breath.)*

◐ I breathe in an energy of joy. *(Take a breath.)*

◐ I breathe in an energy of creativity. *(Take a breath.)*

When saying the mantra, it is not just about saying the words; more importantly, embrace the energy of stillness, courage, joy, and creativity. Truly feel the energy and accept the new choice. Repeating the mantra strengthens the acceptances and the positives as below:

**Stillness** embraces a sense of quiet within.

**Courage** creates stability.

**Joy** gives you energy to create.

**Creativity** lights up the brain.

## Notes

*Like a magician, you have created an illusion. The brain sees the illusion, perceives its confines, and lives within them.*

# Chapter Seven
# *Inaccuracies of Thought*

It is a cloudy, overcast day, and a strong wind whips the sea into action, causing white horses to form. It roars and rages in the distance. My mind mirrors the confusion depicted in these unsettled conditions, and the turmoil within me reflects the turmoil outside. I gaze out to the horizon, where the storm clouds are brewing, to reflect on past emotions and my inner world, a combination and expression of my life experience. I have come to the conclusion that I am the author of my own story, and only I truly know what is written within the pages. Its complexity prohibits a quick conclusion to inner issues, because each issue has its own beginning and end. The length in between has intricate twists and turns, each with its own hidden depths and layers. This weather has a beginning and an end.

This chapter looks at how your response to everyday situations can move you to sink to various depths emotionally. Everyone has the potential to experience great joy, yet so many people are disabled by their past that they are unable to experience it. These beliefs are seen as real truths by you today and will move you to repeat a similar pattern of behavior—until one day, you pause to think, to analyze at a deeper level, what is actually happening in your life.

What part do you actually play in shaping your present reality? Living your life under a fog of illusion and not being aware of the intricate web that you are weaving will lead to disappointment and disillusionment.

This is where the disparity in your thinking occurs, because you can be directed by inaccuracies. Emotions will veil your judgment and cause you to make decisions that do not really work for you. A deep-seated hurt creates vulnerability, and the mind will continually drag you back along familiar lines of experience and feeling. One thought can, in an instant, trigger an immediate response on mental and emotional levels, bringing to life a past emotional experience.

Traumatic experiences can drive you to sink to a deep, low level within yourself. The stronger the emotional experience, the deeper you will sink.

This is very similar to digging a well ten meters deep; the more spades of soil you remove, the deeper the hole. Some people live life with a good base of stability. They will only move between levels one to three emotionally, and they'll never experience or truly understand the turmoil felt by others who plummet to a deep level of ten. A heightened negative emotional experience will have been disturbing and emotionally challenging. It will push the individual to a deep level within the emotional core. The base of stability shifts as their emotional boundaries expand.

If this has been your experience, you will find that once this road is travelled, it is very easy to follow the same pathway again. Instead of moving from level one to two and then moving slowly to the next level, in which case you would have a greater chance of stopping yourself sinking deeper, you fall instantly through the energy layers. You will move directly from one to ten, which is an old, familiar place, and you will easily re-experience a hurt once lived through. As you venture back and sink into these emotions, over time you reinforce the apparent validity of the experience.

The mind is very complex. If a thought is connected to a strong emotion, the thought has more power and potency. Dr. Kerry Spackman, a renowned neuroscientist and author of The Winner's Bible, states, *"A crucial step in surviving a tragedy is to break this endless repetitive cycle of thoughts because repetition only wears you out emotionally and keeps your initial emotional response going long after it should have stopped."* Dr. Spackman has worked extensively with motor racing champions, Olympic and world champions, and businesspeople. In his book, he outlines his research and guides readers to start their own personal winner's bible.

## *Mental versus Physical Tiredness - My Own Experience:*

I was driving to Central Otago, New Zealand, excited to have a few days away. It was a warm, sunny day, and I was full of optimism. A few hours into the journey, a great sense of tiredness enveloped me, and I sank into that feeling. As the mind and body connected to this energy of tiredness, so did a mental belief that everything seemed so hard, difficult, and overwhelming.

I felt myself drop deeper in that moment. After stopping the car at a country fruit stall to buy some fresh produce, my focus diverted to what was on sale and the newness of my surroundings. It wasn't until I returned to the car that I noticed I no longer felt tired, and life no longer seemed so difficult. This situation brought to my awareness that the tiredness I was feeling was a mental tiredness, which felt like a physical reality. It was a mind-set, a product of thoughts and the energetic memory held within my mind.

My dear mother held a great tiredness within her; she was born into a family of eight and had ten children of her own. She never let it hold her back but would push herself to the point of exhaustion.

I recognized that this tiredness was also derived

from the family line, a link to my mother's experience. From that day on, if I became tired, I would ask myself, "Is this a true physical tiredness, or a mental tiredness that is connected to the past?" I made a choice to stop myself sinking into the energetic memory and to let go of the thoughts that were driving the emotional feeling. I took control. When tiredness arose, I would say, "I acknowledge my tiredness, and I acknowledge that I have an abundance of energy for all my requirements." In time, this emotional experience left me, and my energy and vitality grew.

If I had allowed myself to sink into the feeling that life is too hard, the energy would have overwhelmed me. I would then have had to live out the emotion attached to this energy, which in turn would have radically affected my holiday experience.

Moving beyond your past and breaking this repetitive cycle requires a willingness to change and an understanding of the patterns you created in the past and how they impact you today.

## *Strategies to Deal with Emotions*

- Reclaim control by using your mind to control your emotions, and don't let them dictate to you. You do have a choice: either sink into your emotions and let them rule your day and your life, or take control.

- The onset of the emotion is the best time to make your move. If you allow yourself to sink deeper, it will be increasingly difficult for you to get out of the emotional feeling.

- If you do sink into your emotions, you may sink a long way. You will be taken through the same feeling and emotion. You will become stuck in the emotional experience of the past, which has been triggered by the present. Keep a record in your journal if this has been your experience.

- Divert the mind from focusing on negative thoughts and dwelling on the past. Focus on something else.

- With practice, taking control and diverting yourself will become easier.

## *Find Out What Works for You*

Here are some extra tools to divert the mind from sinking into and reliving old emotions.

- Talking to others helps dissipate emotions.

- Read a book, soak in a bath, or focus your attention on a practical task around your home.

- Watch a TV program or do something for someone else; divert your attention from yourself.

- Go out for a walk. Take time to be in the moment. Focus on your surroundings, the trees, the plants, bird life, or the ocean. Take time to just be in the moment.

- Meditation can support you to still the mind, snap the mind from its focus, and energize the body. It can support you to take control.

- Exercise breaks down emotions. Emotions are chemicals; when you sweat, you are releasing emotions.

◯ Go out and play. Connect with positive people and have a good time. Don't forget that laughing is good medicine.

# Notes

# Inaccuracies of Thought

*You cannot change the facts, in the script of what has been, but you CAN change the affect that the past has on you today.*

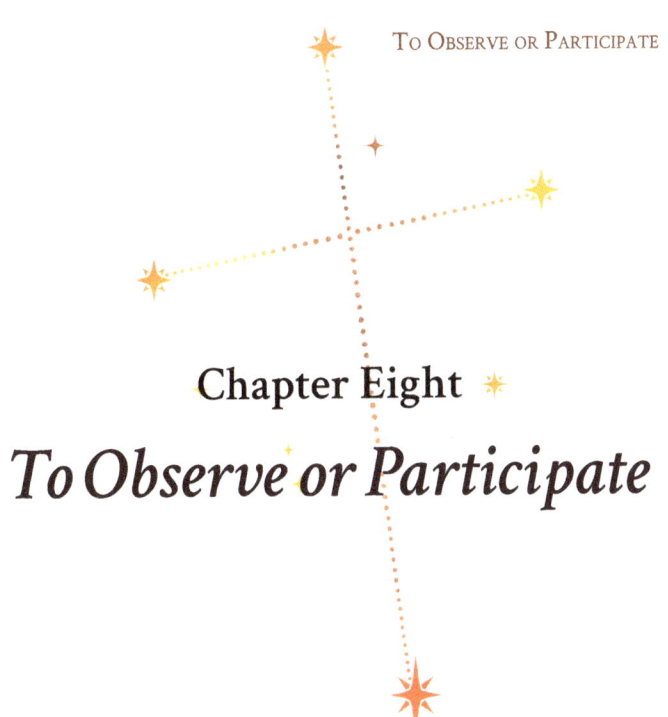

# Chapter Eight
# *To Observe or Participate*

### *Stephen's Experience*

Stephen went to work feeling generally happy. However, later that day he felt extremely annoyed; a feeling of anxiety throbbed inside him and caused great discomfort. No thoughts stirred in his mind as the nervousness dominated. He thought back over the day and found that he had mostly worked alone, except for a short meeting in the morning.

He did recall having a minor difference of opinion at the time, but he couldn't see how this was connected to what was happening now. Stephen's difference of opinion had actually triggered the energy thought and emotion from a past experience, and so he relived the same emotion again on this day.

Why he was initially annoyed in the present was placed on the periphery as the old emotional response took control, fuelling his experience. This is a common occurrence for many people. The key in Stephen's case was to observe himself, acknowledge his thoughts and feelings because these are clues as to what is at a deeper level, not participate in the emotional experience by sinking further into the anxiety, and focus on his work, which acted as a distraction.

If you take the time to reflect on your own life, do you have a history of sinking into your emotions? Or do you repeatedly find yourself being pulled into someone else's emotional drama, full force into a conflict situation? Clearly seeing what you are doing can create a light bulb moment. Clarity is an important key to change. One useful technique if you feel drawn to conflict is to imagine yourself stepping back, one step at a time, until you can observe without being overwhelmed.

Remember we are all ultimately responsible for our own lives and choices. You may want to protect a loved one and try repeatedly to make their life easier, but it is not always possible to succeed. The other person has to gain insight into their own behavior and, until this happens, nothing will change for them. My experience shows that, for some reason, certain people aren't ready to make changes and sometimes the timing isn't right. Therefore, if you choose to wait for the other person to change, you will become anchored in their reality instead of your own.

Making changes in how you relate and what you will or will not accept, presents others with an opportunity to also change. You are not responsible for the other person's happiness. If you find that you get caught up in feelings of guilt, sadness, or blame, acknowledge the feeling, make a choice to let this pattern go, and choose a new positive choice that will empower your life.

If you choose not to, you will both end up in a stalemate situation by continuing with your old patterns of behavior. These patterns will surely dominate the landscape of your life.

## *Mindfulness—Walking Meditation*

I started yoga and meditation with a Tibetan yoga master, Kunga Tsering. My teacher had an amazing way of looking at life, and the meditation room had an incredibly serene energy.

The following walking meditation will support you to take your focus off repetitive thinking and bring you into the living moment.

- Breathe deeply and slowly, and relax. Allow all tension and careless thoughts to drift away.

- Become mindful of your experience while walking; focus on placing one foot in front of the other.

- Don't focus your eyes on anything in particular. I generally look toward the pathway or straight ahead.

- If your mind wanders, bring your mind back to the present, to your steps and breathing.

- I have found that even if I do this for a few minutes at a time, my focus can become completely centered on the here and now.

↻ The more you practice this meditation, the longer you will be able to stay in the moment. This enables your mind and body to relax.

## *To be in a place of Stillness or Quietness*

I am a great believer in meditation and mindfulness. However, for some people, being in the moment is not necessarily a happy mode of being as they have yet to find a sense of inner peace. Below is an explanation of the difference between being in a place of stillness or quietness:

There is stillness and there is quietness. In stillness, there are no emotions, while in quietness, there are emotions. When you are still, you are in a place of peace. In this place you will find your answers and find your wisdom. When you're in quietness, you can be in a place of fear or another emotion. It can be a dark place where there is not a sense of the future; there is just a sense of the past pressing down upon you.

Everyone has a natural stillness but very few actually find it. Everyone has quietness, but not many can find the way out. One can do so through understanding what is contained in that quietness. Understanding creates a pathway to the stillness, and once you've found it, you'll never lose it.

## Notes

*Life is a matter of choice. I choose to prosper, to be aware, to be strong, to be adventurous and safe. I choose to be happy, to be confident.*

## Chapter Nine
## *The Will*

The spirit created the mind, the mind developed a personality and the personality influences what is deemed the will. The will can be likened to a book of instructions collated through many reincarnations that enhance in this life your good points or bad points.

The will influences ambition, and therefore you may carry the ambition to do nothing or to succeed. The will is a complex driving force; it can take you to the highest peak of your potential. For anyone to develop to the fullness of themselves, the will as much as the mind and the personality must be healed. In other words, the whole person.

## *Jane's Battle*

Jane has good insight into herself and her past, yet one morning she slipped back into a familiar place where her emotions took control.

Jane lay in bed, physically unable to move; it was as though invisible hands were holding her down. Her mind was in a battle with her will, which dictated that she stay in bed, in safety, even though she knew this was harmful to her emotional well-being.

This was a familiar pattern, and yet today this behavior was more visible. Jane told herself to get up and enjoy the day, she and tried to move, but she still felt that she could not. "Why is this happening?" she asked herself. She knew that she had to break free from the emotions that had the power to hold her, as if paralyzed, in her body. Jane recognized that she had sunk deep into her emotions, and she felt captive!

Ten minutes passed, which felt like hours, until suddenly her mind clicked into a new awareness with profound clarity. This empowered a belief that she controlled her mind and her ability to move physically and emotionally. A new determination surfaced, and she forcefully said, "No more. I will get up!" Jane harnessed all her mental strength and flung herself out of bed. She jumped in the shower.

She was truly amazed at the power of her mind and the emotions that had overwhelmed her, convincing her to believe that she was unable to lift her head. She went out of the house and walked, thinking about and analyzing what had just happened. She reeled in the realization of the power of her mind.

Jane had made the choice to not lie as a victim to her emotional turmoil, and she could see with absolute clarity how her thoughts and emotions had influenced her experience and created her reality.

Through letting go of the past and changing her thinking, Jane strengthened the conscious mind, which in turn empowered her choice to not give up. This marked a turning point in her life unlike any other—a profound moment that she will never forget.

It is important to reclaim control over your emotions; otherwise, it can be like riding a wild horse and not having hold of the reins. You will be driven relentlessly until it stops of its own accord.

## *Notes*

*Serenity is the stillness of knowing that you belong not just in a small picture, but in the big picture that is Creation itself!*

# Chapter Ten
## *The Void*

You may not understand what is happening in your life and feel only half alive, drifting through the day with the occasional pocket of joy. You may feel disconnected from the inner you and notice that your daily routine exists to prioritize the needs of others. This in itself can bring you to ask yourself, "Where do I fit in the scheme of things?"

If something is missing in your life, you may come

to realize that this something could be you. There are various roles you will undertake in your life that may take precedence over your own personal aspirations. For example, the role of spouse, the role of parent, or the role of provider may have dominated your life so far. The inner needs of the woman or the man may have not been given priority.

By losing sight of your inner self, the happiness you desire will continue to elude you. You will merely move through the motions of life rather than truly participating in the joys. A lack of connection to the whole self creates a void. The connection to life is merely routine as the true self has disappeared.

At various life stages, you may seek to redefine yourself, to set out new guidelines on how you choose to live your life. You may have outgrown old habits and routines, or you desire a complete change in direction. Possibly your inner growth may not match your present life situation. This may occur at a new life stage, or when the children leave home, after a relationship breakup, or at retirement—to name some.

If you want to create a different life, you have to set about changing your original guidelines and kick out old patterns that keep you locked in routine. Living a life that does not provide you with adequate stimulation will become uninteresting allowing boredom to flourish. Did you know that boredom can affect your energy levels, creating a form of tiredness? The outcome of this is that it will be harder for you to motivate yourself.

## Carol Breaks Free

During the time that I worked in Community Mental Health, I met Carol, a woman who had been through an emotionally abusive relationship. Her husband had dominated her married life and would not allow her to make decisions, and she disclosed that she truly feared the repercussions. Carol had three children who had been home-schooled according to her husband's wishes. The entire family had never socialized in the community and were kept in semi-isolation.

Carol had felt trapped for many years, until one day she summed up enough courage to leave. It was a year later that I made an appointment with Carol and went out to see her at her home. My main role was to support her to reintegrate more fully into the community, working from a strengths-based perspective to support

Carol to improve her quality of life and gain confidence in her ability to make decisions for herself.

On this particular day during our conversation, I realized that Carol continued to feel very stuck. She had a safe home for herself and her children, and the relationship was over, yet she was still held back by old patterns. She disclosed that her husband had even dictated the way she should hang her clothes. She told me that she continued to leave some clothes in a suitcase because in the past, she never knew when her husband would move them. On top of that, she had always left a few things packed in case she got the courage to leave. She felt stuck and couldn't think of what to do next in her life.

She didn't understand what was happening to her. Her mind was stuck in a place of confusion. She had no new guidelines of her own to follow, no idea of what to do. She was waiting for someone to tell her what to do. The mind had created a stalemate. She didn't know how to move on, and her mind could not come up with an outcome, a possible future. She had to redefine herself and set new guidelines for how she would like to live her life now.

With understanding herself better, Carol was able to

see beyond her present situation. She came up with ideas of how she could make small but positive movement in her life. I encouraged Carol to write a list of what was important to her and what was not. How would she like to live her life? How would she like it to be? Initially, Carol looked at small changes, and as her confidence grew, she moved on, now able to let go of old, crippling beliefs. She set new guidelines for herself and her family that were supportive and flexible. Over time, Carol was able to make positive and lasting changes.

## *Redefine Yourself and Reassess Your Life*

Start with the basics. For example, you may want to be treated with greater respect, or receive more support or recognition for what you do.

- ↺ What changes would you like to make—in relationships, personal goals, career, or material possessions?

- ↺ Look at options. Do some research and also consider something that you have never tried previously or never believed that you could achieve.

- What are the steps to get you there?

- Prioritize. Look at daily, weekly, and long-term goals. Regularly review and revise your priorities.

- How can you enact these changes? Again, set yourself a time frame. Consider what needs immediate action.

- Most important, place yourself first and enjoy the process of getting there.

# Notes

*I connect to life by connecting to myself: within me is a wealth of positive emotions, of love, of passion, of creativity, and serenity. I am whole; I feel the good and the positive within myself.*

## Chapter Eleven
### *Diving Deep*

I have written 'Diving Deep' to support you on your journey. Please note, however, that this information should not be used to replace professional help.

Diving deep looks briefly at the effects of rejection, abandonment, and trauma on the inner level. This is an incredibly difficult and sensitive topic for many people. I would like to support you on your journey to free yourself, to move beyond the past and to create a fresh start.

If this chapter triggers you emotionally, it may be because you are reconnecting to a deep hurt within you. I suggest that before you read this chapter, form the following intention: "I choose to release and let go of old hurts and emotions that rise to the surface, to the conscious mind." Then accept the following: "I choose to replace the emotions released with the energy of love, peace, and joy."

A traumatic experience accentuates a belief of not being safe in the world, and it develops a heightened state of sensitivity and vulnerability. Depending on what has been your experience, your emotional boundaries will usually expand, as discussed in chapter seven; this allows you to sink to a deep level emotionally.

The inner child is strongly affected by the experience, and the mind can become stuck in a state of shock. Over time, your emotions ebb and flow with varying intensity, deep within the energetic layers with feelings of anger, embarrassment, helplessness, and self-blame. You can also experience underlying feelings of guilt, shame, powerlessness, panic, fear, aloneness, or sadness. The emotional impact of the past is carried in the body.

Scientific research shows that a person enters a state

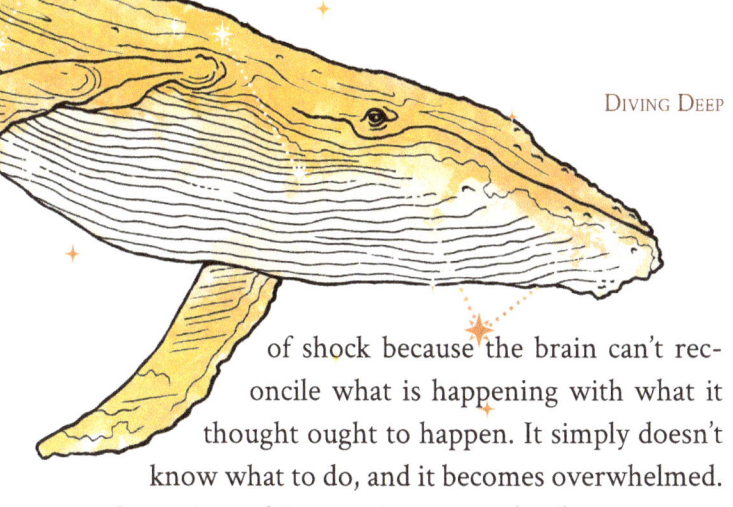

of shock because the brain can't reconcile what is happening with what it thought ought to happen. It simply doesn't know what to do, and it becomes overwhelmed.

Over time, this experience can develop a pattern where the individual separates from their own emotions, a form of disconnection, which was developed as a way to distance them from an intense experience. This is seen as a way to cope, to survive. As the years pass, a part of them can become locked in the past, stuck in the emotional experience, which remains active on a deeper level. If emotionally triggered to return, it can feel like a very scary place to be, feeling like there is no way out.

Some describe a sensation of having no protection from the world around them, and of being physically impacted when in the presence of others.

The experience may create a need to strive to control life, and to be overly cautious or vigilant in an attempt to find a measure of security. Some individuals develop the perception that they are "stupid" for putting themselves in a vulnerable position, even though they had no choice.

Unmet needs and expectations will continue to seek to be met, developing an inner longing for what they haven't had. They may make attempts to attract someone or something to fulfill this need. The thoughts, emotions, and acceptances are locked within memory, and they will continue to give their power and control to the past.

You may believe that you have no power to make a change. You do have a great inner strength, which has enabled you to live through what has been. You can move beyond your experience and heal the past in order to reconnect to the wealth of life, the richness of life.

I am here to tell you that it is not your fault.

- ↻ Please choose to accept that it was not your fault; there is nothing wrong with you.

- ↻ Give back the responsibility to others for their own behavior and actions.

## *A Good Affirmation*

☯ I am safe. I trust myself to keep myself safe.

☯ I am worthy. *This creates a sense of worth, creating an expectation of being safe in the world.*

It is very important to create a positive home environment. The inner child and the adult need to feel safe and secure in order to enable them to trust in the world again; in doing this, it will strengthen your courage to step forward.

## *The Little You*

This is a visualization to support you to bring the inner child from the past.

Can you see your way to opening your arms to the little you? Can you open your heart to lift the inner child from the bleakness of the past, in order to find stability in the present?

You may have worked on your past through counseling and feel that you are at the right stage to consider the following visualization.

Visualize yourself walking toward yourself as a child. You can visualize someone there to support you, if this helps. Take the little you by the hand, or lift the child into your arms. Talk to the little you; explain that it is not his or her fault. Let the inner child know that you are now all grown up, that you love him or her, and will protect him or her. Carry the little you, or walk forward together, closing the door behind you. Don't look back.

Sometimes the child may not want to come with you and may require some convincing to leave the perceived safety of the hideaway. Remember to think about what is happening with your thoughts, your emotions, and your body. If it brings up fear of a person in the past, you can imagine shrinking the person to a very small, tiny person—smaller than a mouse.

Remember that this person has no power over you now. The main key is taking back your power and control over your life.

It can also help if you have a picture of yourself this time. Take the time to look at the photo. If you don't have a photo, imagine yourself as a child, and choose to send love to the little you.

The love fills the child, soothes and nourishes, and surrounds the child. Begin to praise yourself regularly; the inner child and the adult need love and self-acceptance, gentleness, kindness, and the warmth of good support and encouragement. They need to know that they are special and are valued.

## *Make a Choice*

- Choose to give yourself a voice. Your needs are important, and you are important.

- Learn to accept yourself, to praise yourself, and to recognize the good within you.

- Allow yourself to receive what is positive; what is beautiful, and what is right for you.

## *Praise Yourself and Give Focus to the Positive*

⟲ Look at the positives in your day.

⟲ List positives about yourself. Are you a kind and caring person? Do you support your family, partner, children, neighbors, and community?

⟲ What are your strong points? Are you patient, kind, intelligent, witty, reliable, punctual, a good listener, supportive, determined, a good worker, and easygoing? Do you have good problem-solving skills?

⟲ Make a commitment to cultivate positive self-praise and love. It is extremely important to acknowledge your achievements no matter how small.

⟲ Take the time to pamper yourself, relax, and do something you enjoy.

⟲ Open the door for others to support you.

## *Innocence*

The energy of innocence contains five elements.

1. **Wonderment** creates an appreciation of beauty.
2. **Faith** that you can do anything, and it makes a difference.
3. **Serenity**—the stillness of knowing you belong not just in a small picture but also in the biggest picture, creation.
4. **Joy** comes out of knowing that you are beautiful.
5. **Love** of oneself.

Make a choice to reclaim the energy of innocence lost in your childhood by reaccepting the five elements above. Then imagine the energy moving toward you and gently settling in your heart center.

This energy creates a continuous, effervescent form of energy that bubbles with life. It allows the inner child to connect to the affirmation, "I'm safe, and the world is safe." In rebuilding the inner child, you rebuild the adult and nurture positive emotions. This will strengthen your choice to break free from the past and walk forward in a new and positive pathway.

# Notes

*When we follow the soul's map, we are meant to pick up messages or clues in the life that we live. If we don't pick up the clues, then we keep coming back – 'reincarnation'.*

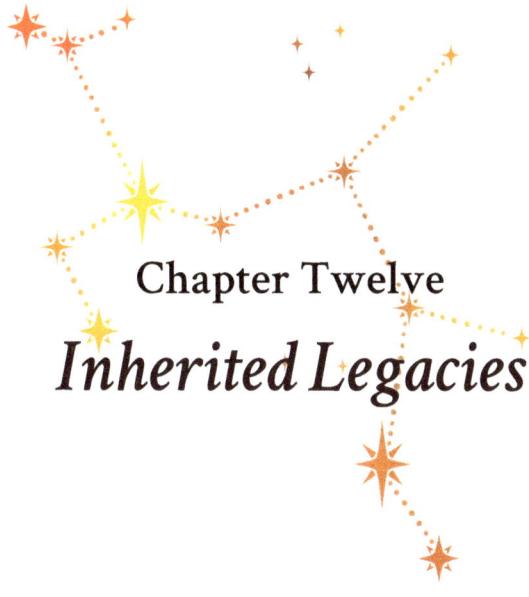

## Chapter Twelve
## *Inherited Legacies*

Decrypto is all about energy. It's about parallel worlds, your conscious reality, your subconscious reality that entwine and separate on a regular basis. Energy is within you and all around you; you are giving and receiving energy on a daily basis. Your thoughts and emotions influence this living, vibrating, energetic world. You have a base energy that is unique to you.

It is my interpretation that from the moment of

conception, we are influenced by the father's and the mother's energies. We experience life in the womb, physically and energetically. The mother's thoughts, emotions, and experiences wash through the unborn child; you could say that this is your first school of thought.

Family members can have similarities and differences, although through your mother's and father's genetic lines, you can be predisposed to certain behaviors, addictions, fatigue, anger, and so on. I have found that adults and children can also have attachments of energy that intermingle with their own individual energies and impact how they think, feel, and react.

Not all members of the same family will carry the same attachments of energy. These predispositions can influence your state of mind and opinion of yourself, and it can fuel your emotions and experience. In the case of anger, your own energy of anger may be like a gentle breeze, but combined with anger from the family line, it may become a swirling tornado.

In regard to an addictive legacy, hereditary factors can predispose you to certain addictions. It is as if you inherited a base of energy, the seed of addiction, which creates a craving that tempts you to need a certain thing.

You then build on this through your own experience. The legacy predisposes you to this, but it does not necessarily mean you that will take it up; it will take more effort on your part not to. You can also inherit strengths or weaknesses. These patterns can be lived out as if they are your own. For example, a belief that life is very difficult, or an inherited tiredness, or (on a positive note) a very strong belief that life works well and things come easily.

## *Working with Children*

Mothers who were concerned about their children started contacting me. I have included two examples below that outline the healing sessions for young David and Peter.

## *Two-year-old David*

When I work with children, I mentally link to the child through the parent. The child does not have to be present during the healing. I can then read them, and I look under the rock that covers what they create in order to see what is important to them and what is troubling them. I locate any issues that are holding them back, causing behavioral problems, lowering their self-esteem, and preventing them from enjoying childhood. To children, their little issues are genuine problems.

Ava was having difficulty managing her two-year-old son, David, who was becoming angry and destructive in his behavior. At the time, I had not worked with a child of this age. I was very surprised to find an attachment of energy linked to his energy, which had the maturity and strength of an adult's energy. It was explosive, abusive, and angry. I described the characteristics of this energy to Ava, who informed me that this was very similar to her ex-husband's family, predominantly in the male line. I came to realize that a child can inherit a particular legacy, an attachment of energy, which predisposes the person to be susceptible to certain behaviors. I had not expected to find an attachment of energy like this in one so young.

As a healer, I have an ability that allows me to move energy from an individual who has given me permission. I do this by clearing the energy from the person, moving it into myself and out through me. I then gently heal in order to settle the emotion and create a greater sense of stability and self-confidence within the child. The awareness of David's inner world and the background issues affecting his behavior allowed Ava insight into his behavior, which supported her to manage everyday situations, as well as parent more effectively.

Some months later, Ava rang me to let me know that there was a marked change in her son; he was just like a two-year-old should be and had not reverted to the previous behavior.

## *Three-year-old Peter*

Olivia was experiencing difficulty with her three-year-old son, Peter. He had very strong issues around eating, which would send him into panic, fear, and high emotion. The family had tried all sorts of avenues to no avail, and this situation caused turmoil for everyone.

Peter would only eat certain foods, which was very limited with no fruits or vegetables. He would continually experience strong emotions and panic around eating. Peter had seen a psychologist, who advised that the best way to deal with this situation was to step back and let her son eat what he wanted.

During the first session, I connected to two past lives, where there were issues around food. In the first life, he was around eight years old and had had an abusive father who had forced him to eat and was emotionally abusive and threatening.

When I connect to this life or a past life, I feel within myself the child's emotions, distress, and fear. In the second life, he was around nine years old and was terminally ill. He was in a hospital room and had difficulty eating due to illness and medication.

The energy of the trauma was very strong within the body. Both lives created a mind-set of caution within Peter, as well as a great stubbornness and determination. Olivia told me that Peter would watch others from a distance and had anxiety about participating in new things. It took a lot of persuasion and a lot of tears to get him to attempt anything new.

During the first appointment, we touched on both of these lives, looking at how they were played out in this life and the influence they had on his reactions today. I supported Peter by moving the energy and extreme emotion that was connected to these lives. I then healed, settling the heart, the mind, and the body.

Several weeks later, I saw Olivia for a second

appointment. I discovered remnants of the second life—the child in the hospital room. This past life had created in his current life a general anxiety about life and a fear and expectation that his life would be short. The child in the past life had a fear around what happens when death occurs. What would happen to him? Normally, during a session I step back in part from the emotions of the person, because the emotions can be very intense and can cloud my clarity. It was very difficult to do so on that day. I was truly, deeply touched by the emotions within the child in the hospital room. I had to pause and couldn't respond for several minutes.

We looked at accepting new choices for this life, and in so doing, I could feel Peter's mind-set shift. It brought forth to his conscious mind a great reverence for life and a passion to enjoy this life. An appreciation for the small things, that in a previous life, he had not lived long enough to experience.

This was a powerful insight and image. It humbled me and fueled my own reverence and wonder for life. I marveled at how amazing it is that a child, who had suffered in a past life, was gifted with a new life where he was born to positive and loving parents with an opportunity to truly live again.

Peter gave me a great gift, which I will never forget because it is etched firmly in memory. It is ever present, a reminder of how special the gift of life is, and a reminder of the importance of appreciating the moment.

## *E-mail from Olivia*

Two weeks later, I heard back from Olivia. She wrote,

*Hi Linda,*

*Thank you so much for working on Peter last week. I have noticed some small but amazing changes in him. The next day, he was asking for some money, and I said I would give him some if he was good. About half hour later, I said I would double it if he ate something new. I left it up to him to choose what it was.*

*About half an hour later, we were at the shops, and he said could it be fruit. I said, "Sure. Go get what you want." He picked out an apple. On returning from the shops, I cut up a small part of the apple the way he wanted and got my phone ready to record what happened, mainly because I knew my husband wouldn't believe that he ate it. With a big smile on his face, he took a small bite and then another. I managed to get him to eat four small pieces—totally unheard of by him, and with not a tear in sight. Amazing is not a strong enough word.*

*We have had no other huge milestones, but I am sure that he will continue when he is ready. I cannot thank you enough. Just this little step has been great.*

# Notes

## Inherited Legacies

*I receive what is necessary to enrich knowledge, my potential and my purpose. I live to receive what is right for me, to nurture myself, to cherish myself, to award myself. I receive first then I give, then I receive again. I create good balance, good harmony.*

# Chapter Thirteen
# *Emotions and Health*

Positive thoughts and positive emotions are critical to the health of your overall mind. The activity of the mind is also influenced by the activity of the emotions.

## *Something More to Contemplate*

The brain is a living organism and is the most alive part of the body. It is as complex as the star system and yet as simple as a sponge. The brain is physical, the mind is not. The brain has governance over the physical body and the emotions have governance over the mind. The brain is totally impersonal; it is the tool of the mind and the heart "the emotional center". If fear is the ruling emotion in the heart then it severely impacts on the mind and shapes the personality.

The personality of the mind then sends messages to the brain and the brain creates the reality, the experience. If you feel strong emotions of anger, the mind sends the message to the brain and the brain lifts up the fist and you go into battle, it simply follows orders.

During my intuitive healing work, I often find that if a person has unresolved emotions they surge directly from the heart center to the brain and flow back and forth, creating static like disturbance in the energy on the inner level. Over time, these strong and unresolved emotions may cause a glitch, an anomaly, to occur in the brain, which can manifest as a physical symptom. This can create impairment in the functioning of a specific area in the physical body—for example, your knee, liver, or heart.

Each area of discordance releases an energy that limits the brain. Negative emotions severely distort a healthy energy flow in the brain and from the brain to the physical body. The glitch is diagnosed as a physical fault, however the fault is the end result of negative thought combined with a negative emotion.

Obviously there are many reasons why people have physical health issues, which are not connected to emotional issues. My point here is that carrying old baggage into the future may impact on your health.

Getting to know yourself is part of the process that can bring you to create the change you desire. In relinquishing and letting go of the thought, you minimize the emotion with the intention to diminish a fault within the body.

Positive emotions have a powerful effect on your physical and emotional well-being, supporting you to maintain health and vitality as well as empowering you to create positive change.

# Notes

## Emotions and Health

*You know your past as it is in your present. In knowing the present you can change the past, to engineer a new future.*

## Chapter Fourteen
# *Leave the Past Behind*

There may be times in your life where you feel stuck and become stalled in the past. If you fall into a pattern where you constantly dwell on the past, your focus will be on what you have failed to create, on mistakes or regrets. It will tend to be based on disappointment, not success.

Dwelling can drag you into the sadness of life, into a place of defeat, disempowerment, disillusionment, and sorrow. Negative thought, combined with negative emotion, build in strength over time unless you decide to take the time to resolve the issue.

This energy vibrates at a lower frequency and will lower your energy levels. You may recognize if you have felt in a low mood that your energy levels and vitality feel compromised. This in itself can weaken your resolve to move forward. As you will have one foot cemented in the past while you repeatedly attempt to step forward in your life, it is the emotion that compels you to look back.

Life will continually reflect your mind and bring to your attention, in everyday interactions with others, a reminder of what you once had or do not have, of what has been lost, and so on. Unresolved issues can be like carrying a festering sore on your back, which will weep and crust.

It's a constant reminder of what you have been through. If you feel strong emotions toward another—for example, hate, anger, rage, bitterness, or resentment—this energy will have a powerful reaction on your physical and emotional well-being.

According to Dr. Kerry Spackman's author of The Winner's Bible's research – *"...if you don't learn to get over disappointment then you'll end up getting stuck in the past, forever going over the same fateful event. This will cause a cascade of real physical changes to occur in your brain and your body, which will actually physically age you."* \*

What happens in this case is that you lock your mind in the emotional feeling and keep yourself captive by holding onto the emotion. On the inner level, your energy is dense, clouded, and still, like a stagnant pond. By holding on to powerful, negative emotions, you actually punish yourself and allow the past to continue to control you, affecting your ability to find any form of peace in your life.

Deep within yourself, you will know that the past cannot be changed; what has been has been. As hard as this is to accept, the reality is that no amount of dwelling, yearning, or sinking into strong emotions is going to change it. Consider letting go of your past or it will continue to affect you. Forgive and lay to rest past issues, or else they will continue to shape and dictate your life. Life is for living today.

**\*Spackman, Dr Kerry. The Winner's Bible – Rewire Your Brain For Permanent Change. The Winner's Institute, LLC 2009. Atlanta, GA, USA.**

## Notes

## Leave the Past Behind

*I am in control of my present and my future. I create with my power of control. I create what is right for me. I am in control.*

## Chapter Fifteen
# *Relinquish and Rechoose*

When I first started this search many years ago, I was introduced to the concept of relinquishing and rechoosing. I have utilized this method to resolve many past issues, and I continue to do so.

## *How You Can Use This Method*

It is important to formalize letting go of negative thoughts, emotions, and learned patterns. The word relinquish is a special word. It has a resonance, a sound that has the power to bring the brain to attention. When relinquishing, you can speak this out loud or read it to yourself: "I choose to relinquish ..." followed by the thoughts and the acceptances and emotions that you wish to let go of.

Refer to your Journal (started in chapter four) and look at what you have identified as key thoughts, repetitive patterns, and emotions that no longer work for you. The emotions will have no need to resurface when there is resolution and the past has been laid to rest. Making a choice to forgive, with an acceptance that what has happened can't be changed and a choice to move on, will be of great benefit in supporting your desired change.

Once you begin to relinquish and let go of the past, the mind alters and will bring to your awareness how the relinquished patterns and acceptances have actually influenced your life. That which is underneath, at a deeper level, will eventually surface and allow you to see more clearly what has been contributing to your behavior.

After relinquishing, simply breathe gently for ten minutes in silence. This in itself quickens the change within by soothing the energy, the aura. The choice is yours; bit by bit, you can choose to chip away at old thought patterns and choices by relinquishing negative thoughts and emotions and by replacing these with new, positive choices of how you would like your life to be.

## *How to Start*

Sit in a quiet place, where you will not be disturbed. Relinquishing and re-choosing is better if repeated. You can do this at least once a day for several days, up to a week. Continue for as long as you feel necessary; use your own judgment. Remember that deep-seated patterns will be entrenched within the mind; you will need determination to create change.

## *How to Decide What to Relinquish and Rechoose*

- Observe yourself and your interactions with others.

- Seek to understand yourself, identify key thoughts and emotions, and repeated patterns, as discussed previously.

- Get to know your emotional charges. With sadness, fear, defeat, or anger, ask yourself, "What is the emotion trying to express?" If you get angry, have you felt unheard, unacknowledged, not listened to, or treated unfairly?

- What is your body telling you? Are you tense, tired, or anxious? Does your stomach churn, and so on?

- What are your regrets and disappointments? Do you feel guilty, disillusioned, or resentful?

- Can you see emerging patterns? For example, do you feel powerless with an inability to take control?

- ↻ Are you stuck in your life, reliving the same situation over and over again, year after year? Think about what is the possible link to the past, the trigger.

- ↻ If so, write in your journal what your situation is and why you aren't changing it.

Be mindful of the thoughts that float through your mind on a daily basis, as well as what you think or say in conversation with others. All are clues to what is hidden in the subconscious.

## *Important: Replace the Negative with a Positive*

Always replace negative thoughts with positive thoughts. For every negative emotion, there is an opposite, a positive emotion. You may not feel the new choice reflects you at this stage. Remember that this is what you are moving toward and choosing to create in the present and in the future.

If you do not replace the negative with a positive,

you will be diminishing the negative without building a positive in its place—and so you will leave a void.

In accepting positive choices and new guidelines, you are building a solid foundation of stability in the mind and the emotional center. This will give you strength and allow you to reconnect to positive emotions within yourself; generally, you'll feel happier and can enjoy life. You will be raising your energetic vibration, which will attract more of what is positive and good.

## *Some examples of Positive Rechoosing*

- ↻ I choose fully to connect with life. I choose fully to participate in the positive, in the joys of life.

- ↻ I accept that life is smooth, easy, uncomplicated and successful, I move forward.

- ↻ I choose to accept that good flows to me, connects to me. Good things always happen to me.

- ↻ I choose to accept that I believe in myself. I

believe in my right to receive what is good, what is right.

- ↻ I believe I deserve the best in the here and now.

- ↻ I create with ease my goals and my dreams. I laugh, I play, I love, I explore, and I'm fine.

- ↻ I choose to accept that I create a flow of money. Money flows to me.

- ↻ I create financial wealth with ease.

- ↻ In the place of anger: I choose to accept that I create serenity in my life, joy, happiness, and ease. I relax, I am calm, and I move forward.

- ↻ In the place of self-dislike: I choose to accept that I am learning to love myself, to be kind to myself, and to see the good in me.

✦

The following relinquishing and re-choosing exercise has been written specifically for anyone who has been the victim of abuse.

## *Please Choose to Relinquish*

- A choice to never forget.

- A constant reminder to never drop your guard. The reminder was needed because of a belief that if the person trusts someone, then the person will be abused again.

- Please choose to release the energy of the victim. Otherwise it will continue to disempower you.

- Visualize the energy moving from you and toward the ocean, or imagine blowing the energy into various colored balloons, tie them at the ends, and see them move upward towards the sky and far away.

## *Please Choose to Accept*

- I no longer require a reminder; my wisdom will keep me safe. My wisdom and my intelligence will say whether or not it's right.

- I'm safe and protected. I can relax and be at ease. I'm safe. (You will need to repeat this choice many times to reinforce this acceptance.)

- I strongly reclaim control and authority over my own life.

- I am in control of my present, my future.

- I create with my power of control. I create what is right for me. I am in control.

- I believe in myself, in my right to receive what is good and what is right.

- I move forward. I create positive change. (You will need to repeat this choice many times to reinforce this acceptance.)

## *Sarah's Outcome*

A situation arose that made Sarah feel anxious. She had many things to do and was not sure how she was going to complete them. There was an anxiety about getting it all right. During her childhood, she had unknowingly created a list of things that she believed she had to accomplish. This made her vulnerable to anxiety as an adult, and she would unconsciously feel anxious about her ability to fulfill her own list of requirements.

The expectations that Sarah had set for herself were as follows.

1. *I must get it right and so do it right.*
2. *I have to do it by myself. I'm on my own.*
3. *I must be nice and thoughtful.*
4. *I must be vigilant, be aware, and do it before it needs to be done.*
5. *I must be completely together. I can't frown or be angry.*

In this case, Sarah relinquished the childhood choices. For example: "I choose to relinquish the following acceptances: I must get it right, do it right, and so on." You can also choose to relinquish an energy of anxiety about completing this list. Make another list, reversing all the patterns and thoughts into positive choices. You then choose a positive, new emotion to replace a negative emotion.

Sarah chose the following acceptances to replace what she had relinquished.

- I choose to accept that I may relax in heart, mind, and body, in the awareness that I am supported. I can be guided to ensure that what I have to do is done. I grow in strength, in confidence. I relax, and I'm fine.

- I choose to accept an energy of stillness, of ease, to replace the anxiety. *One method is to close your eyes and imagine this energy floating toward you and filling your body. You can then state the intention to seal the energy within yourself.*

Sarah had to keep periodically relinquishing and reaccepting the above. She found that being aware of what was driving her behavior was invaluable. If she started to feel anxious, instead of being pulled deeply into her emotions, she was able to observe herself and acknowledge her feelings. Sarah would then look at what she really needed to do on that day and what could be left.

Over time, the anxiety lessened considerably, and she felt stronger and calmer in herself.

# Notes

*I give myself permission to be happy, to be free, to pursue my own dreams, to fulfill my purpose. I create what is best for me, I prosper, and I grow.*

## Chapter Sixteen

# *The Power of Manifesting*

There is perfection in the moment: walking along the beach, wading through the shallow surf that surges at my feet. The sun's warmth is blown by the gentle breeze; it caresses my face, and joy arises. I marvel at the beauty of nature and the serenity that builds within me. Life indeed feels grand, and in this moment, I am wealthy. The sound of the waves crashing onto the shore is music to my ears and soothes the senses.

## *My Life*

In my early years, I built walls around myself and confined myself within fenced parameters, not unlike an animal in a paddock, held in by an electric fence. At the time, it was hard to see how my life could be different. It was as if all my goals and dreams were planted in arid soil and failed to sprout into life.

I then believed that I was doing all I could to create change and that life dictated to me. I convinced myself that I was dealing with my past and working toward making changes, but I realize now that I wasn't truly actualizing these changes into reality. I stood still as life passed me by, and I continued on with the same routine, growing increasingly bored and unhappy within myself.

I was caught like a fly in a spider's web: the more I struggled, the more the web encased me. Then one fine day, I stopped struggling and accepted that this was my life. In acceptance, I continued on in the same way day after day, feeling trapped. However, now I feel free. Even though I am with no job or income, I'm sitting here and being creative with two passions, writing and the sea. The money from my house sale subsidizes my freedom. I question, "Why aren't I nervous and making an attempt to fly back into the web, to be entangled once again into acceptance of my routine life that did not give me a sense of fulfillment?"

I finally flew out of the spider's web after ten years in the same job in New Zealand. I made a choice to move to Sydney, Australia. I believe this was a direct result of working on my past life and experience, which allowed me to grow in confidence with increasing certainty. In a way, this created a desire for a major life change and precipitated the decision to make this move. My partner, Ivan, has a sense of adventure and was happy to go along with my choice. Moving to a new country is a big undertaking because in some ways, one has to start again and rebuild a new life. This adventure propelled me to accept change and to acknowledge any remaining insecurities that arose during this time.

Interestingly just prior to this move, while still in the security of my job and living my familiar life, I felt very positive. Working toward my goals was fairly easy for me. When it came to the day that I was ready to hand in my notice at work and book our tickets, a strong feeling of fear surfaced, to the point where it felt as if all the hair on my head was standing on end. At the time, this was a shock to me, and I remember thinking, "Gosh where did that come from?" This was a good lesson for me as I realized that it must be the same for many people who are secure when they are moving toward their goals, but on an inner level there is a strong resistance that can prevent them reaching the final stage of manifestation. Regardless, I had a stronger determination to move in the direction of my choice.

For several months after moving to Sydney, we viewed many apartments on the rental market. I had no real income myself and planned to use the money left from the house sale in New Zealand to pay for expenses. There were many apartments available that were far away from the sea—dull, uninspiring places to live in, and many on busy roads. This time was set aside to live a dream and move in the direction of our choice, as well as truly break free from restrictions that I had previously placed upon myself.

It was eight months later that I realized how very important our decision to move would prove to be. In fact, it could have saved our lives. We had inadvertently escaped the Christchurch earthquake. Ivan's apartment had been in the central business district, and my work had required me to drive through Christchurch on a regular basis.

We had made a choice to make a change, and this choice has now created a different future for both of us.

We signed up for an apartment with an amazing sea view, which was a perfect place for me to write this book. In making this choice and allowing my dream to become a reality, a new world opened up and changed our pathway. This choice enabled me to see how very powerful it is to live one's dream. Once again, I am near the ocean and close enough to see and feel the soothing rhythm of the waves surging to the shore. It is like feeling bereaved and then being reunited with a loved one. How strange it is to love something that mimics emotions, one day calm and the next day tumultuous. The ocean doesn't feel, and it doesn't actually care, but its mere presence soothes and touches one's inner soul, one's inner being.

Suddenly, a part of my life once again felt complete. Inadvertently, the door that I had shut many years before, after my sailing adventure from New Zealand to England, was opened again. Looking out to the ever-changing blue ocean, so expansive and limitless, gives the feeling of once again being on a yacht, totally embraced by sea.

In allowing myself to live my dream and achieve that which really makes me happy, I am rewarded in ways that I could have never have imagined. Now the ocean fuels me, uplifts and inspires me, and stimulates my creativity and desire to write—hence the notes that you are reading today. I cannot emphasize enough what a powerful concoction it is to see, to feel, and to taste an achievevment.

When you create an environment that activates a feeling of joy and completeness, life becomes much easier. Your preferred environment will continually lift your energy and fuel your positivity.

An action creates a reaction, so seize opportunities to activate change and move forward to create your goals and dreams. Make a choice and allow yourself to make your dream a reality. To live your dream is very powerful and facilitates a greater sense of health and well-being. The joy experienced in creating a vision into reality is truly magical indeed.

*I embrace what is positive within me, to create what is right for me. I choose to be truly alive, truly vibrant, truly me. I am boundless; I am free to be me. Anything is possible. I can do it. I can achieve my goals and dreams.*

## Chapter Seventeen
## *Dream Big*

Have realistic and obtainable goals, and also keep a space where you can what I call Dream Big. You may have been dreaming of a possible future but have no idea at this stage how you can bring it about. This dream may seem out of your reach.

Allow yourself to dream and open the door for opportunities to come to you. Allow the universe, fate, or destiny to start to work. If you shut the door to possibilities, there is little chance of realizing what you desire.

An example is with The Voice talent show in Australia, where the contestants had no idea a year ago that their lives would change so remarkably. Some of the contestants talked of having no singing experience and only singing in the shower before they were given an opportunity to audition on national TV.

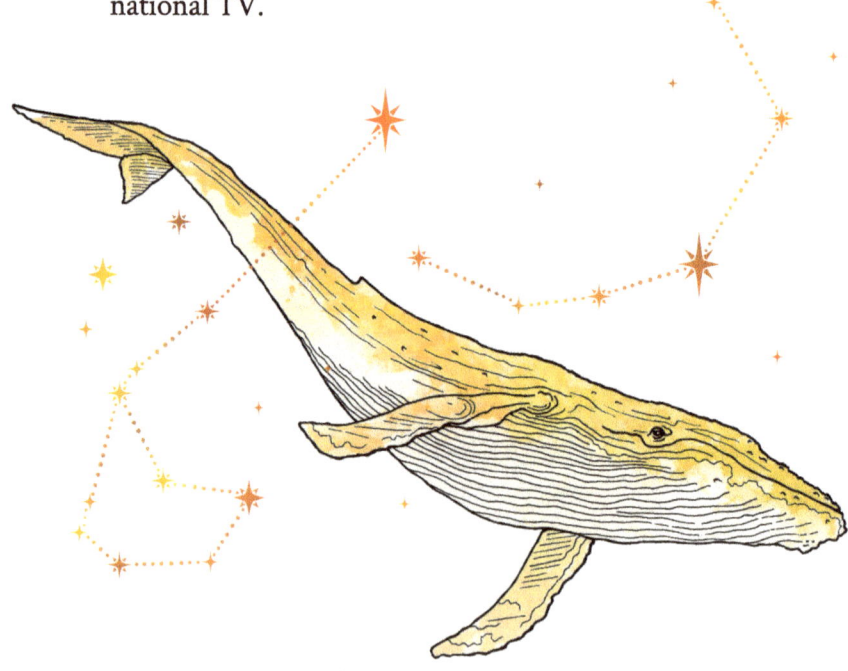

They then went on to spend quality time with stars such as Ricky Martin and Will.i.am. The decision to enter the competition dramatically changed their lives. They started with an idea and looked for an opening to explore this idea further, and they made their vision a reality by auditioning for the program. When performing live, they had to dedicate time and energy into perfecting their performance and developing a true belief in their ability to succeed under the mentorship of world-class stars.

## *Create a Dream Catcher*

Have you found that when you talk to others about a goal or dream, they have various points of view? At times, it may cause you to doubt yourself and your idea. The doubt and negative energy from others can deflate you and cause an energy drop, and you will lose the power to create successfully.

Create yourself an energy dream catcher. Choose to surround your dream with optimism and positivity. Simply choose to say the following.

- ↺ I create a dream catcher to surround me and my dream or goal. Anything negative from others is discarded before it touches me.

- ↺ What passes through is bright and positive.

Your dream will have a greater protection from the influence of others, although in saying this, you have to continue to be positive and put energy into manifesting your dreams and goals.

## *Empower Positive Thought*

By the time you reach this chapter you will be on you're way to creating a new vision for your future. It is very important to put energy into manifesting the desired change and altering the way you live your life in order to suit these changes.

Your new choices are like new shoots of growth and need to be nurtured and strengthened, as they have not yet been actualized. New pathways have not been laid down. They are ideas that lay dormant and inactive, awaiting an action on your part. This can take time, but moving forward, being fulfilled, and experiencing satisfaction are truly possible for you.

With resolving and healing the past, you are also strengthening the conscious mind, and empowering your ability to manifest your goals and dreams. In turn, this builds a greater sense of peace within you. With peace comes stillness, which is a true wealth that no amount of money can buy.

I have found the use of affirmations and regularly visualizing does empower me and strengthens my resolve to move ahead and create the change that I desire.

Dr. Kerry Spackman, in *The Winner's Bible- Rewire Your Brain For Permanent Change*, promotes that if visualization is done correctly, this will develop new circuits in your brain. Your brain will then release additional neurotransmitters as you activate your senses and emotions during visualization. The more you practice visualizing your goals, the more you reinforce and strengthen a positive emotional response, which in turn empowers your choices.

Your mind develops the thought. If the thought is strongly laden with emotion, then that thought will take precedence over other thoughts. The stronger the emotion, the more the thought moves ahead to be created.

This voyage of discovery into the depths of yourself will continue as long as you want it to. You will need courage and determination to move forward and to make the change that you desire. Keep focused and forge ahead, and you will get there!

## *Notes*

# About The Author
## *Linda K. Ford*

Linda lives in Sydney, Australia, and has worked guiding others for over 20 years as an Intuitive Speaker/Healer and a Social Worker.

Her love of the ocean is the inspiration behind her writing, which was strengthened during a 15-month sailing adventure, from New Zealand to England in the 1990's. Some years later she wrote and published her book 'Caution to the Wind'.

Passionate about supporting others who are in search of answers to better understand themselves, and the life they have created, Linda guides them to achieve clarity and the self-awareness required that instigates life-altering change.

You can get in touch with Linda by visiting her author website or by contacting her through Facebook using the links below.

*www.facebook.com/lindakfordauthor*
*www.lindakfordauthor.com*

# More From This Author:
## *Caution To The Wind*

On May 5th, 1994, at 9.30 am on a chilly, sunlit day, Linda Ford and Geoff Wright, left the safety of Lyttleton Harbour in New Zealand, to venture into the unknown, where nothing would be predictable.

The voyage plan was to follow the famous trade wind route, sailing from New Zealand to England.

All too soon, they found themselves battling their way to Sydney, Australia. Caught in a ruthless storm with no contact with the outside world, they were truly alone. All the romantic notions of the ultimate cruising life disappeared into oblivion.

Step aboard Ebony and take an adventure, an epic 15-month voyage. Experience the day-to-day passionate tale, packed with intrigue, and at times suspense. Experience the delights of the lands visited and learn more about the world of international sailing. This was a life changing adventure, with a dramatic, unexpected, ending.

**Available from: www.lindakfordauthor.com**

www.ingramcontent.com/pod-product-compliance
Lightning Source LLC
Chambersburg PA
CBHW062059290426
44110CB00022B/2645